5D Thinking

Workbook for Kindergarten

Science Secrets
in 5 Steps

Discover Signs of God and Develop Sound Character

HARTFORD IIK PRESS

HARTFORD IIK PRESS

Prepared by 5D Thinking Team

Dr. Necati Aydin

Uzma Ahmed

Saba Irshad Ansari

Design By:

VERA | FiKiR SANAT

Print Date:

November 2023

Table of Contents

HARTFORD IIK PRESS

Seeing the Signs of God in Science in 5 Steps

1 EXPLORE

facsinating facts without falsehood

Delve into the wonders of the universe using science. Present fascinating scientific facts. Filter false ideologies.

2 COMPARE

Wonders of the universe vs. man-made wonders

Use analogy to reflect upon the wonders of the universe side by side with man-made wonders. Highlight that both require intention, knowledge, and power.

3 QUESTION

Negate nature, material causes, and chance as the source

Reject prevailing notions that attribute the universe's marvels to mother nature, material causes, or blind chance. Use comparisons from the previous step as a foundation for this inquiry.

4 CONNECT

Point to interconnectivity and dependency. Perceive Divine Names and signs (ayah).

Point to the intricate web within the cosmos—its interconnectivity and interdependence. Demonstrate that all things are united like one entity and rely upon each other due to their innate impotence. Conclude that only the One with infinite knowledge and power could be the Maker. Finally, relate the gained knowledge to the Divine Names.

5 APPRECIATE

Offer sincere gratitute through dhikr, fikr, and shukr

Cherish (shukr) God's creations by remembering (dhikr) that they are the intentional gifts of God. Reflect (fikr) upon their immense value and our deep dependence on them.

CHARACTER

After the five steps, link the signs (ayah) in the universe to the relevant verses (ayah) in the Qur'an. Highlight the exemplary Prophetic practices (sunnah) in relation to these signs. Conclude with character lessons and heartfelt prayer (du'a).

Why 5D thinking?

Science seeks to uncover the causes behind our ever-changing universe, explaining these transformations and suggesting ways to influence them. In the secular worldview, the existence of all phenomena is credited to material causes, nature, and chance. The materialist ideology within this perspective breaks the bond between creation and the Creator, ascribing existence solely to nature, cause, and chance. This embedded ideology in modern science blinds individuals, preventing them from discerning reality. We must shed this 'materialist ideology' to truly appreciate scientific knowledge. Then, science can guide us to the genuine reality of the universe.

The dominant secular perspective implies that science and the concept of a Creator are distinct domains that shouldn't intersect. The Tawhidi worldview challenges such a separation, presenting an integrated approach to perceive the genuine reality, emphasizing the indispensable link between creation and the Creator. The 5D Thinking Model, grounded in the Tawhidi worldview, attempts to illuminate this connection and interpret the messages embedded in creation. Integrating the 5D Model into primary science education can pave the way for a richer understanding of the created world, fortifying a bond with the Creator.

Muslim educators are entrusted with the challenge of surpassing materialist ideology, adopting a structured methodology that empowers students to forge a relationship with their Creator. The 5D Thinking Model goes beyond merely referencing Qur'anic verses and Hadiths; it proposes a unique approach to decode the messages in the universe's book by interpreting its symbolic signs (verses).

The 5D Thinking Model boasts the following distinctive features:

First, it will eliminate any explicit or implicit assertions that causes, nature, or chance are the true sources of observed phenomena. By removing the blindfold of learned ignorance in the secular perspective, students can marvel at God's extraordinary and dynamic creative acts.

Second, the model uses an analogy to make subjects understandable and relatable. This approach is rooted in the belief that the heart is the ultimate repository of validated knowledge. Through analogy, new knowledge can be verified and accepted by the heart with certainty.

Third, it fosters critical thinking through questioning, helping students sift through false choices and arrive at the correct answer through their reasoning.

Fourth, it reassures students that the correct choice is evidence-based and verifiable. This dimension allows them to understand why God must be the sole creator of the observed phenomena.

Fifth, it helps students recognize the infinite value of the observed phenomena and appreciate the importance of this gift for them and other beings in the universe. It also guides them to derive moral and character lessons from scientific topics.

This framework gives students the tools to know God intimately, personally, and meaningfully. They are encouraged to interact with the world in a manner that consistently unveils God's ayah (signs) in His acts. As the Qur'an suggests, they are steered to associate these divine acts with His revered names. This relationship amplifies their connection and communication with God, turning every revelation into a journey towards perceiving the Divine names and attributes.

How to use 5D workbook?

Each chapter follows a framework to guide the students through a 5-Step journey.

First Step – Explore

Begin by immersing your students in the topic to captivate their interest.

- Present scientific knowledge without referring to **causes, natural laws, or chance** occurrences.
- Be mindful of your **word choice,** as it reveals the underlying worldview. Use words like **designed**, created, and **made** to set the mindset towards the idea of a Creator.
- **Avoid terms** that suggest that material causes, nature, or chance are the origins of the phenomena under discussion.
- Present relevant videos and discuss the content. If any video hints at a secular ideology, point it out.
- Highlight **Fascinating facts** that will spark curiosity and ignite a passion for exploration.

Second Step – Compare

Now, transition to the second dimension where you'll encourage your students to compare the explored phenomena to a man-made one for better comprehension.

- Encourage them to come up with an analogy.
- Draw parallels between the explored phenomena and human-made objects to uncover profound **analogies**.
- Use the video to engage in thoughtful **comparisons**.
- Highlight the **similarities** and **differences** between Created and man-made phenomena.
- The goal here is for students to grasp the concept of creation using their understanding of man-made objects.
- Make sure students understand the amount of knowledge, power and will behind

both explored and man-made phenomena.

Third Step – Question

Here, you'll shift into the role of a mentor who challenges conventional thought.

- Urge students to **contemplate the origins** of man-made objects concerning nature, causality, and randomness.
- Help them realize that man-made wonders arise from **knowledge, power, and intention.**
- Stimulate critical thinking by **questioning the concept of nature,** which comprises particles, energy, and physical laws, yet lacks consciousness and intent.
- Illustrate that **material causes** (which consist of material parts/components) do not, on their own, cause things to grow or change.
- Debunk the notion of **sheer chance** or randomness.
- Revisit analogies from the earlier step to strengthen your negation of **secular trios.**
- Discuss the "who", "what", and "where" of the man-made entities in question.

Fourth Step – Connect

Venture into a dimension where students **witness the marvel** of the Creator's handiwork.

- Highlight the complex **interrelatedness** of the observed phenomena and present evidence pointing to a Maker.
- Delve into discussions about the **interdependency** found in creation.
- Initiate conversations on the **beneficial outcomes** of created entities, showcasing the benevolence of their Creator.
- Conclude that such a Creator must possess **infinite power and wisdom,** referred to as Allah in the Qur'an.
- Encourage students to suggest **Divine Names** inferred from the topics discussed.

Fifth Step - Appreciate

This dimension emphasizes **gratitude and introspection**. Lead your students to unearth deeper meaning and lessons from the topics explored.

- Help them discern the intended benefits of observed phenomena and recognize their significance as **special gifts.**

- Engage in **Dhikr**, highlighting how the topic evokes thoughts of Allah as the only possible Creator.
- Practice **Fikr**, reflecting on the profound wisdom and power behind the explored phenomena.
- Express gratitude, or **Shukr**, for the observable blessings in Allah's bounty.

Engaging in this dimension will help students extract moral and ethical lessons, encouraging them to embrace these gifts fully, instilling a sense of purpose and virtue.

Character Lessons

The 5D model doesn't just prioritize academic learning; it promotes moral reasoning and character development. Its primary goal is to nurture individuals aware of their cosmic position and their connection with Allah. Instead of treating science as a standalone subject, students learn to view it as a medium to deepen their understanding of the world and self, discovering moral lessons and deep meaning embedded in a scientific perspective.

Qur'an and Hadith

Relevant verses enable students to recognize overlapping messages and meanings in the Qur'an and the universe. Relevant Hadith remind students of the teachings of the Prophet (saw) as an all-encompassing role model.

Activities

This section offers a variety of activities for each of the 5 Dimensions, empowering educators to tailor them to their students' needs and capabilities. These engaging activities reinforce the lessons delivered through the 5D model.

Think Thank Game

General Instructions

The Think Thank Game is a delightful and gratitude-filled activity designed to help students appreciate the countless blessings of Allah. Played in groups of at least two, the game involves one player expressing their thankfulness for a specific aspect of the given topic following the prompt "Alhamdulillah!" The player must complete ten rounds without any pauses or repetitions to win the game. This interactive activity fosters appreciation and a deeper understanding of the wonders surrounding us.

Example for K-1 Grade - Alhamdulillah for the Human Body:

Moderator: "Alhamdulillah! (loudly and fast)."

Player (One player, ten rounds):

"Alhamdulillah for the eyes to see!"

"Alhamdulillah for the ears to hear!"

"Alhamdulillah, for the hands to touch and hold things!"

"Alhamdulillah for the nose to smell flowers and yummy food!"

"Alhamdulillah, for the feet to walk and run!"

"Alhamdulillah for the skin to feel touch and sensations!"

"Alhamdulillah, for the heart that keeps us alive!"

"Alhamdulillah, for the brain that helps us think and learn!"

"Alhamdulillah, for the bones that give our body structure and support!"

"Alhamdulillah, for the mouth to eat and talk!"

My Amazing Body

Learning Outcomes

After this lesson, learners will be able to:

- Name their body parts.
- Understand that their body cannot make itself.
- Understand that Allah made their body.
- Learn some names of Allah.
- Know their body is a blessing.
- Learn some character lessons from the topic.

Look in the mirror.

What do you see?

Two bright eyes, one cute nose,
Ten wiggly fingers, ten little toes.

Soft, round cheeks, a smile so sweet,
Hands to high-five and tapping feet.

Video:

Fascinating Facts

Body Part	Cool Fact
• **Eyes**	They blink 20 times every minute!
• **Ears**	They keep getting bigger!
• **Tongue**	It has 8,000 tiny taste spots!
• **Nose**	It helps with tasting food!
• **Fingers**	Your fingerprints are unique, just like you!

2 Second Step — Compare

Let's compare a toy doll to your body.

Dolls have heads, arms, and legs.

Some are made of plastic in a factory.

Some are made of cloth.

How are dolls different than you?

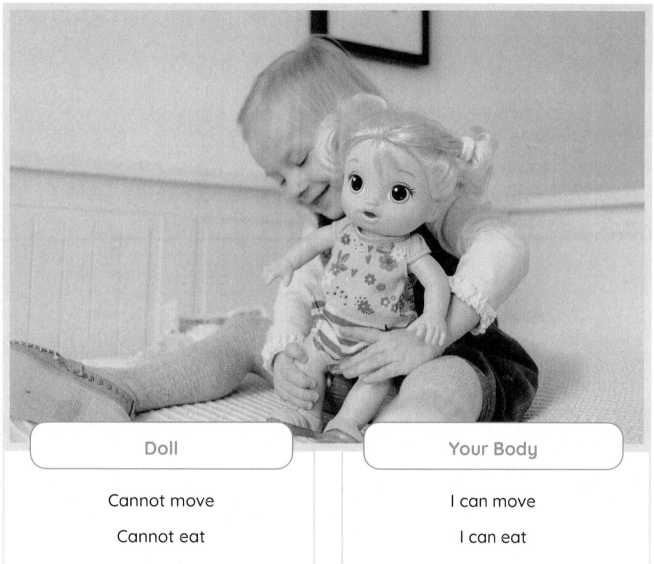

Doll	Your Body
Cannot move	I can move
Cannot eat	I can eat
Cannot sleep	I can sleep
Cannot talk	I can talk
No feelings	I have feelings
Cannot grow	I can grow

Who made your body?

Can your body make itself? No, it cannot.

Did you get two legs, two feet, two of everything by accident?

No, you did not.

Let's think together:

- What do we need to make a doll?
- How is a doll made?
- How many people work to make dolls?

People make a doll. Who made your body?

Teachers notes:

Facilitate discussion with these questions: Let's compare your body and the doll. Which one is better? Which one is more beautiful? Do you know how your body grows? It needs energy from food and water. But can food and water make your body grow? Why can we make a doll which could grow? You know that someone makes a doll with knowledge and ability. Then, there must be a Maker of your body as well. If all humans come together, they cannot make a human body because they have limited knowledge and power. So, who is the Maker of your body? How is a rag doll stitched? Do you think the threads, wool, and cloth can use a needle and make a doll themselves? Do you think animals could make them?

 # Fourth Step Connect

What does your body need to grow?

Your body needs food and water.

Where does food come from?

It can be from plants and animals.

Where do they come from?

Plants need the Sun, soil, and water.

So, the maker of your body must be the maker of all these things.

Only Allah can make them all.

Allah gives your body a beautiful shape. He is a powerful maker, giving you many body parts that let you walk, run, play, speak, hear, eat, and much more. Allah knows your body needs water and food for energy. He takes care of the Earth for you to live on. He makes the Sun bring energy and light to plants to grow. He makes the night for rest and the day to work and play. So, he gives everything that your body needs. Whoever makes the body with eyes must also be the One who made the sun and light.

What does your body tell you about Allah?

He knows all the body parts we need.	All-Knowing	Al-Aleem
He makes each body part do different things.	All-Powerful	Al-Qadir
He gives us water and food for energy.	Most Wise	Al-Hakeem
He makes everything to help us live and grow.	The Creator	Al-Khaliq
He shapes our bodies beautifully.	The Fashioner	Al-Musawwir

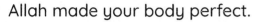

Fifth Step  Appreciate

Allah made your body perfect.

What if your eyes were under your feet?

What if your mouth was at the back of your head?

Allah has made you in the best form.

Your body is a gift from Allah.

Thank him for the gift by looking after it.

Dhikr Think of Allah when you see yourself in the mirror. Only He could make your body.

Fikr Think about how special your body is.

Shukr Thank Allah for your hands, feet, and voice. Use them to do good things.

Teachers notes:

Discuss: Allah is very wise and kind. He's the one who made everything in the world, including our amazing body parts! Let's talk about some of them! He gave us eyes to see all the beautiful colors around us. We can use our eyes to watch the twinkling stars, the colorful flowers, and our favorite toys. Allah gave us ears to hear lovely sounds like birds chirping and our friends' laughter. He also gave us a nose to smell delicious things like yummy cookies baking in the oven or the scent of a beautiful flower. Remember our mouths! We use it to taste delicious foods like ice cream, fruits, and yummy meals made with love. Allah also gave us hands to hug our loved ones, draw pretty pictures, and build amazing things with our toys. He gave us feet to run, play, jump in puddles, and explore the world. All these body parts are gifts from Allah, making us special and unique. We should always be thankful and take good care of our amazing bodies because they help us do so many wonderful things!"

Character Lessons

What can we learn from our bodies?

TEAMWORK:

Your body is like a team. Hands, feet, eyes, and ears all work together. Be a team player!

RESPECT EVERYONE:

Everyone is special. Everyone is amazing. Be nice to everyone!

BE HELPFUL:

Your body helps you do so many things. Help others with kind actions!

Teachers notes:

Our bodies are precious gifts; we must care for them like a trust. It's like when we borrow a nice toy, and we keep it safe and clean. We should do the same with our bodies because they are important and special.

22

Connect with Qur'an

Allah tells us that he made us in the best way.

لَقَدْ خَلَقْنَا ٱلْإِنسَـٰنَ فِىٓ أَحْسَنِ تَقْوِيمٍ

"Indeed, We created humans in the best form."
[SURAH AT-TIN, 95:3]

Teacher notes: Discuss how Allah made us in the best form.

"He created humankind from sounding clay like pottery."
[SURAH RAHMAN, 54:14]

Hadith

The Prophet (pbuh) tells us that Muslims should take care of each other: "All believers are one body, and when one part of the body is hurting, then the entire body is hurting."

(BUKHARI)

Du'a

Two hands to hold and play,
Two feet to run and sway.
O Allah, with this gift so fine,
Help us use it well and shine.

24

Activities

Explore

Match the picture to the words.

hair

head

arm

leg

neck

eye

ear

tummy

knee

foot

See-Think-Wonder

Watch the video about the human body.
What did you see?

What is special about the human body?

How is the human body made?

- Look at yourself in the mirror. What can you see?
- Draw your face on a piece of paper. Look in the mirror to help you.

Compare

Let's talk!

Teacher notes: Facilitate this discussion in small groups.

Can your doll make itself? What about you?

Does a doll's hair grow? How about yours?

Did you make yourself? Who made you?

Thinking Cap

Tick true or false

☐ Your ears do not grow.

☐ Everyone has the same fingerprints.

☐ Did we get two legs by accident?

☐ Dolls are made in a factory.

☐ Your body makes itself from food.

Connect

Draw a picture of the things your body needs. Use the words to help you.

food   water   sun   plants

Color the name of Allah.

Appreciate

Draw three body parts that you are thankful to Allah for them.

Draw a picture.

Share your thoughts with your friends.

Ants in Action

Learning Outcomes

After this lesson, learners will be able to:

- Explore the life of ants.
- Learn that ants cannot make themselves.
- Understand that Allah made ants.
- Learn some names of Allah.
- Know that ants are helpful creatures.
- Learn character lessons from the topic.

Strong ants

Sarah saw ants in the garden.

Some ants carried leaves and seeds.

She watched them go into a hole.

Inside the hole was a big ant home with many rooms.

The ants worked together like friends.

Sarah went inside her house.

She looked at her computer.

She learned that ants live like a big family.

Some ants get food, some help at home.

There is a queen ant, too. Ants help plants grow.

Sarah was happy to see busy ants.

Let's Explore more about ants through this video.

Fascinating facts

Strong Ants: Ants look to be very strong! They can carry very big things

Teamwork: Ants are like friends. They work together to get food and make their home.

Ant Houses: Ants have homes under the ground called nests. It's like a tiny city!

Feeling Feet: Ants don't have ears. They feel things with their feet.

Busy at work: Ants are very busy. They work every day to clean their home and get food.

Watch the video for more facts.

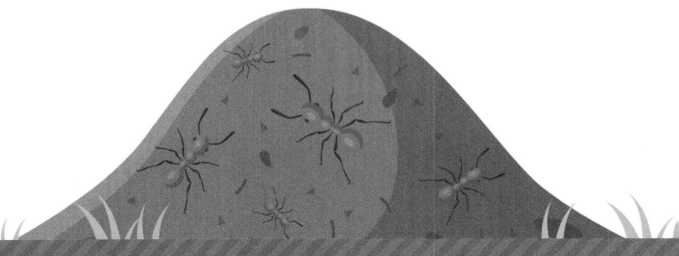

Let's compare ants to a crawler crane.

Ants

- Very strong for their small size!
- They make homes under the ground.
- They can lift heavy things.
- They eat food.
- They talk to each other.

Crawler Cranes

- Very strong, big machines!
- They help people make tall buildings.
- They can lift heavy things.
- They do not eat food.
- They cannot talk.

Both ants and cranes are strong and help build things!
Watch this video that shows how a crawler crane is set up.

Third Step — Question

Let's find out who made ants.

Did ants make themselves? No, they cannot.

Can crawler cranes make themselves? No, they cannot.

Let's think together:

It takes many people to make a big crawler crane.

They use special machines.

They must know how to make them.

Who can make an ant?

Do you think ants were made by accident?

Can scientists make ants?

The maker of ants must know a lot.

Who makes ants?

Teachers notes:

Facilitate the discussion with these questions: Let's compare ants to crawler cranes. Were crawler cranes built by people with the knowledge and power to design and assemble them? Yes, they had so many skills and spent time and energy making them. What about ants with amazing strength, teamwork, and organized colonies? Do they not need a designer and a maker? According to scientists, life for ants begins with the queen ant laying tiny eggs. But where did the queen come from? Then, young ants are cared for by the worker ants as they go through different stages of growth until they become mature ants. But how do ants know how to do that? How do they build their homes and work together so well? We know that people made crawler cranes, but did someone make ants, too? Just like a baby crane doesn't come from eggs, ants have their special way of starting life. So, who is the maker of ants?

Fourth Step   Connect

What do ants need to live?

Ants need water to drink.

They eat nectar and tiny bugs.

They need soil to build their homes.

The maker of ants gives all the things that ants need.

The maker of ants must know a lot. Only Allah can make ants.

Teachers notes:

Ants are made to help improve the soil through tunneling. This produces rich soil, which allows plants to grow. Animals eat plants. So, ants are designed to help plants, trees, and other creatures, thus connecting to them. Is the universe aware of ants, cares about them, and prepares the right conditions for them to live? Or is there a maker of ants who connects ants to other creatures? Do ants want to help because they have good hearts? Or do someone make them to do so? It is only an all-powerful, all-knowledgeable creator who can do this. That is Allah.

What do ants tell you about Allah?

He creates ants.	The Creator	Al-Khaliq
He makes ants strong. They can lift heavy things.	The Fashioner	Al-Mussawir
He gives ants a special job. They help keeping the soil healthy.	Most Wise	Al-Hakeem
He makes the world a place where all animals help each other.	Most Merciful	Ar-Rahman
He knows about every ant working under the ground.	The Aware	Al-Khabeer

5 Fifth Step   Appreciate

Ants are useful helpers.

Ants spread seeds to help new plants grow.

Ants make tunnels in the ground. They help the soil to stay healthy.

They are a gift from Allah.

We should thank Allah for this gift.

Dhikr		Remember Allah when you see ants working hard. He makes them work to get food.
Fikr		Think about the amazing job ants do.
Shukr		Thank Allah for ants. They help soil, plants, animals, and us.

Teachers notes:

Facilitate the discussion with these ideas: We should appreciate ants because they are incredible creatures vital to our environment. These tiny insects work tirelessly together in colonies, showcasing the power of teamwork and cooperation. Ants are designed to play a significant role in keeping our surroundings clean by breaking down and recycling dead plants and animals. They also serve as a crucial food source for many other animals, contributing to the balance of the food chain. Additionally, Allah employs some ants to help plants grow by dispersing their seeds. Their digging activities ventilate the soil and benefit plant growth. Observing ants in action can be fascinating as we learn about their behavior and communication. By appreciating ants, we develop a deeper connection with Allah, seeing his love, wisdom, and generosity.

Character Lessons

Tiny ants teach us.

HARD WORK:

Ants work hard all day. They never give up.

TEAMWORK:

Ants help each other. We must work as a team.

BE TİDY:

Ants keep their homes neat. We must put our toys away to keep our rooms clean, too!

Connect with Qur'an

The Qur'an has a sweet story about ants.

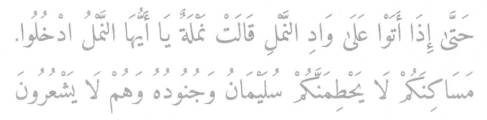

"Until, when they came upon the valley of the ants, an ant said,
"O ants, enter your homes so that you do not be crushed by
Solomon and his soldiers while they do not feel it."

[Surah An Naml, 27:18]

Watch this video about Ants in the Quran.

Hadith

From this Hadith, we can understand that no one can make an ant:

"Allah Almighty said: Who is more unjust than one who considers his creation as My creation? Let him create the smallest ant or let him create a grain of wheat or barely"

(Bukhari)

Du'a

O Allah, thank You for each little ant,

They work so hard, never say "I can't."

Help me be kind to them, every day,

And work hard like them and pray.

Activities

Match the words to the picture.

head

mouth

eye

feet

antenna

thorax

leg

abdomen

See-Think-Wonder

Watch the video about ants and their colony organization.

What did you see?

What do you think of it?

How do you think ants amazing works?

43

Arts and Crafts

- Watch the YouTube video and make an ant farm in a jar.

- Draw or paint an ant or an ant colony.
- Find out about how ants help farmers.

Compare

Let's Talk

How did ants become so strong?

How do ants know how to make an amazing home?

Can ants think? Who made ants?

Thinking Cap

✓ **Tick true or false** ✗

☐ Ants can lift very heavy things.

☐ Scientists can make a real ant.

☐ Ants can make themselves.

☐ Allah made ants to help us.

☐ We must thank Allah for the gift of ants.

Appreciate

Tell your friend three things about ants that make you happy.

Color the name of Allah.

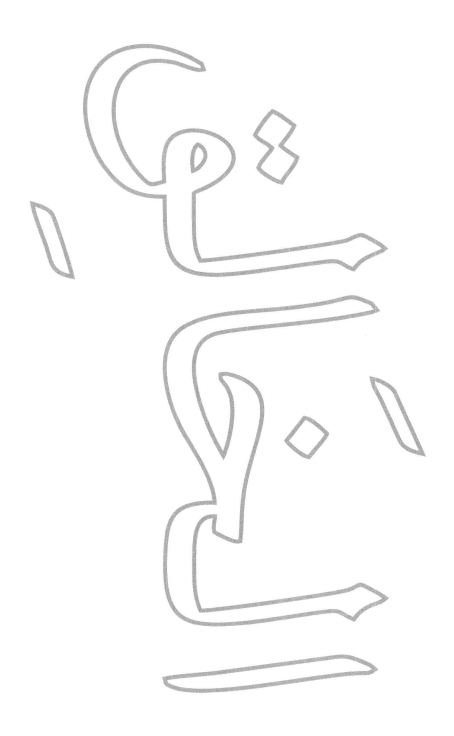

Connect

Draw a picture of the things that ants need. Use the words to help you.

insects   soil   sun   plants   animals

What I learned

Draw a picture.

Share your thoughts with your friends.

Fantastic Fish

Learning Outcomes

After this lesson, learners will be able to:

- Tell about some features of fish.
- Understand that fish cannot make themselves.
- Understand that it is Allah who made fish.
- Learn some names of Allah.
- Know that fish are a blessing.
- Learn some character lessons from fish.

A Fun Aquarium Trip

Sarah and Adam went to see fish with their mom and dad.

They saw big fish and small fish.

Some fish were orange. Some were blue.

Sarah saw a fish with stripes.

Mom said, "The stripes help fish hide."

Adam asked, "How do fish breathe?"

Dad said, "They use gills."

"They all have tails," said Sarah.

"Tails help fish swim," said Mom.

"Some fish have fins. They help fish swim, too," said Dad.

Sarah and Adam had a fun day.

Watch this video to learn more about fish.

Fascinating Facts

Did You Know...?	About Birds!
Fish chat	They can make sounds!
No eyelids	Most fish cannot blink!
Age	Some fish can be as old as your grandpa!
Great memory	Some fish remember who gives them food.
Sleeping	Some like to lay on their side!

2 Second Step Compare

Let's compare a fish to a submarine.

Watch a video about submarines.
Can you make a Lego submarine?
Use this video to help you.

Submarine

What is it?	It is a big machine. It swims underwater.
How does it float?	It needs tanks with air.
How does it move?	People use computers to move it.
How does it breathe?	It does not breathe.
What is it for?	To explore deep in the ocean

Fish

What is it?	Animals that live in water
How does it float?	It has a swim bladder.
How does it move?	It has fins and a tail to swim.
How does it breathe?	It has gills to breathe underwater.
What is it for?	Fish are food for us.

Let's find out who made fish.

Can fish make themselves?

No, they cannot.

Can a submarine make itself?

No, it is made by people.

Let's think together:

- You can make a Lego submarine.
- You need to use your mind and hands.
- The maker of fish must know a lot.
- The maker of fish must have a lot of power.

Who is the maker of fish?

Facilitate discussion with these questions: Can submarine parts assemble themselves into a complete submarine without people? A team of engineers is needed to design, build, and maintain submarines. Skills and knowledge are essential to build submarines and ensure they work correctly. If making a submarine requires this much effort, what about creating incredible colorful fish that are much more complex than submarines? Fish shows us that there is a designer who made them. This Creator knows so much and has the power to make such awesome fish!

4 Fourth Step 🔗 Connect

What do fish need to live?

Fish need water.

Fish need light.

Fish need plants.

We need fish for food. They make us healthy.

So, the maker of fish must be the maker of all things.

Only Allah can make all things.

Let's talk about how fish brings benefits. They are made to keep the water clean by eating dead plants and animals. They also play a big part in the food chain. Some fish eat tiny plants and animals called plankton, while others eat smaller fish, and then even bigger fish or animals eat those fish, too. Humans also eat fish.

Fish are amazing creatures that show us how everything in the universe is connected and play a special role in keeping our world healthy and balanced. Therefore, the Creator of fish must be the Creator of other living beings. Creating a fish requires endless power that is only with Allah. Thus, humans could not make fish. Only Allah makes them.

What do fish tell you about Allah?

He knows how to make fish breathe underwater.

| All-Knowing | Al-Aleem |

He gives fish their wonderful colors.

| The beautiful | Al-Jameel |

He makes fish to give us energy.

| Most Wise | Al-Hakeem |

He makes many types of fish.

| The Creator | Al Khaliq |

He gives so many kinds of food from the sea.

| All-Merciful | Ar-Rahman |

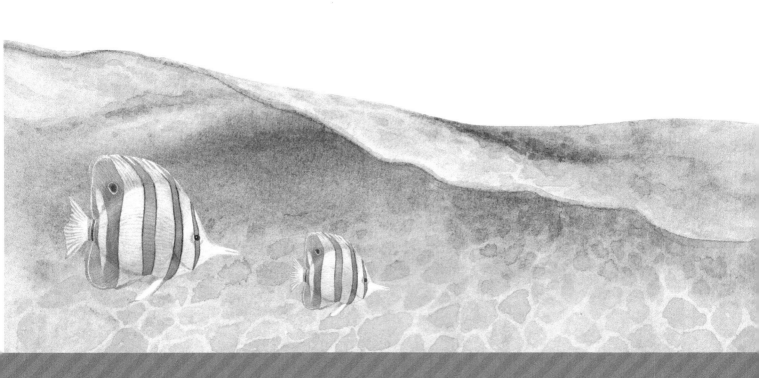

Allah gives us pretty fish. They are a gift.

Fish clean the water.

They are food for birds and other fish.

We should take care of fish.

We must thank Allah for the fish.

Dhikr		When we see fish swim, we remember Allah makes them. Allah is very powerful.
Fikr		Think about how amazing fish are. They have a special body to swim.
Shukr		Thank Allah for the wonderful gift of fish.

Teachers notes:

Facilitate discussion with these points: Discuss how fish is designed to play an essential role in the ecosystem by helping to keep the water clean and balanced. Explain that fish are a crucial part of the food chain, bringing nutrition for many animals, including humans. Highlight their diversity and importance in various cultures as a food source and even as pets in aquariums. Encourage learners to share personal experiences or stories related to fish and discuss ways to show appreciation for fish and their underwater homes by protecting the environment and being responsible caretakers of aquatic ecosystems.

Character Lessons

We can learn some lessons from fish.

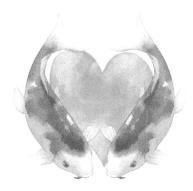

KİNDNESS:

We can be kind. Fish help each other.

TEAMWORK:

Fish swim together. They show us how to work as a team.

BEİNG SPECİAL:

Fish are all different, just like us! It's good to be special in your own way.

Connect with Qur'an

The Qur'an tells us about fish and other things in the sea like pearls:

وَهُوَ ٱلَّذِى سَخَّرَ ٱلْبَحْرَ لِتَأْكُلُوا۟ مِنْهُ لَحْمًا طَرِيًّا وَتَسْتَخْرِجُوا۟ مِنْهُ حِلْيَةً تَلْبَسُونَهَا وَتَرَى ٱلْفُلْكَ مَوَاخِرَ فِيهِ وَلِتَبْتَغُوا۟ مِن فَضْلِهِۦ وَلَعَلَّكُمْ تَشْكُرُونَ

And He made the sea subservient that you may eat fresh tender meat from it. You bring forth from it ornaments which you wear. And you see the ships cleaving through it. And these are for you that you might seek His Virtue and may be grateful.

[AN NAHL, 16:14]

Hadith

The Prophet (pbuh) tells us the importance of knowledge: "Everything seeks forgiveness for the teacher of virtue, even fish in the sea."

(AT-TIRMIDHI)

Du'a

Let's be thankful, for the fish in the sea,

They are gifts from Allah, for you and me.

They are a sign for people to see.

Let's Pray to Allah, to keep them free.

Activities

Explore

Match the words to the picture.

(eye) (mouth) (gills)

(fin) (tail) (scales)

See-Think-Wonder

Watch this amazing video about fish communication through different sounds.
What did you see?

What do you think about fish making sounds?

How do fish gain this amazing ability?

- Draw a parrot fish and color it.
- Working in groups, making sea animals together.

Compare

Let's Talk

Teacher notes: Facilitate this discussion in small groups.

How do fish breathe under the water?

What is it like living in a submarine for a few weeks?

Is it easy to make a submarine?

Thinking Cap

 Tick true or false

- [ ] Fish do not have eyelids.
- [ ] Fish made themselves.
- [ ] A Lego submarine can make itself.
- [ ] Fish are a gift from Allah.
- [ ] Only Allah can make fish.

Appreciate

Tell your friend three fun fish facts!

Color the name of Allah.

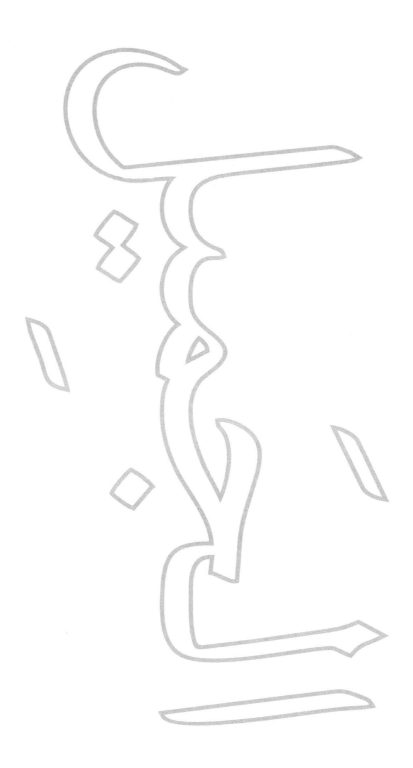

Connect

Draw a picture of the things fish need. Use the words to help you.

food   water   sun   plants

Draw a picture.

Share your thoughts with your friends.

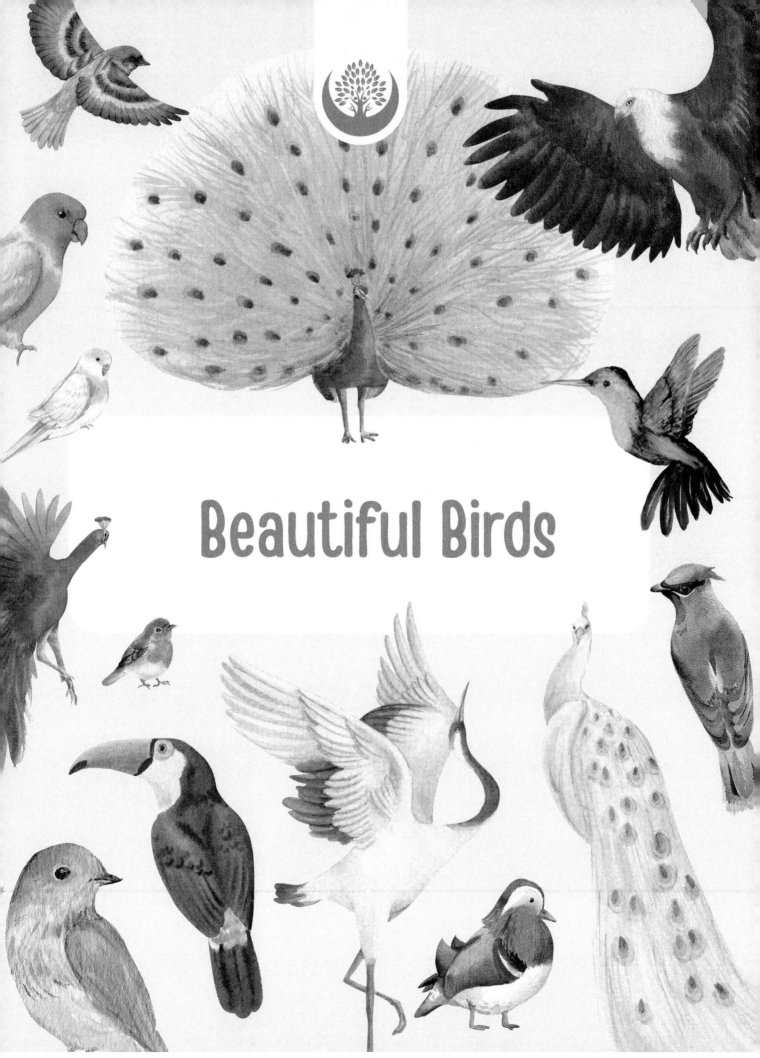

Beautiful Birds

Learning Outcomes

After this lesson, learners will be able to:

- Know that birds are designed to fly.
- Understand that birds cannot make themselves.
- Understand that Allah made birds.
- Learn some names of Allah.
- Know that birds are a blessing.
- Learn some character lessons from birds.

Baby bird wants to fly

A baby bird lived in a nest in a tree.

Mom bird fed him worms every day.

One day, a baby bird saw birds in the sky.

"I want to fly!" he said.

Mom bird said, "Flap your wings!"

The baby bird flapped his wings.

But he could not fly.

"Keep trying!" said Mom.

The next day, the baby bird flew.

He went up, up, up! He was so happy.

Mom Bird was happy, too. The baby bird could fly!

Look at this video of some beautiful birds.

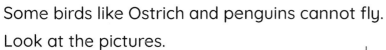

How do birds fly?

Birds have light feathers.

They use their strong chest to move their wings.

Some birds like Ostrich and penguins cannot fly.

Look at the pictures.

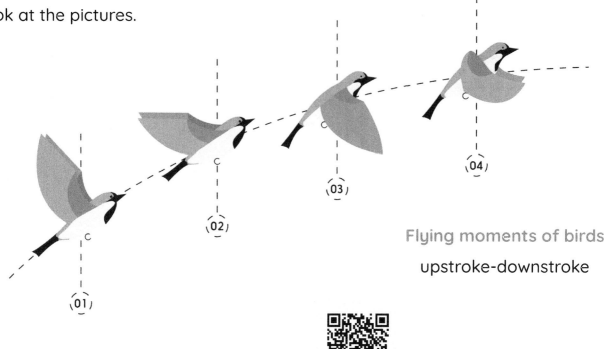

Flying moments of birds

upstroke-downstroke

Watch this video to see how birds fly.

Fascinating Facts

Did You Know...?	About Birds!
Sleepy heads	Some birds sleep with one eye open.
Tiny eggs	A hummingbird's egg is as small as a pea.
Owls	Owls cannot move their eyes.
	They turn their heads almost all around.
Penguins	Penguins swim but don't fly.
Flying far	Some birds go to very far places.

Let's compare birds with airplanes.

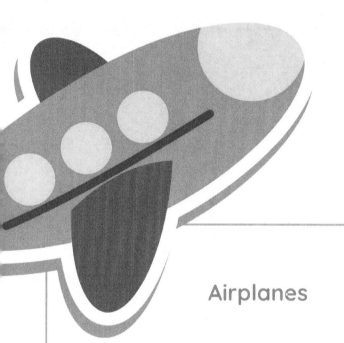

Airplanes	Birds
• They fly and carry people.	• They fly to find food.
• They have wings.	• They have wings.
• They are made from light materials.	• They have light bodies.
• They use engines for flying.	• They use muscles and wings for flying.
• They need a pilot.	• They do not need a pilot.

Watch this video about how airplanes work.

Let's find out who made birds.

Can a bird make itself?

Can a bird know it needs feathers to

Can an airplane make itself?

Let's think together:

- Who made bird wings?
- Who taught birds to fly?
- What makes birds more amazing than airplanes?
- Birds show us someone really special made them.
- The maker of birds knows a lot.

Who made birds?

Facilitate discussion with these points: Imagine you put all the parts of a plane and a guidebook with the steps to build an airplane in a factory. Can all the parts combine and make a jet plane without human effort? Can an instruction manual assemble the parts by itself? A large team of many engineers is required to make one plane. Machines and money are also needed. So, if all this goes into making an airplane, what about birds? Are they not more complex? Do they not need someone to make them?

4 Fourth Step 🔗 Connect

What do birds need to live?

Birds need air to fly.

The sun helps them to know where to go.

They eat bugs to have lots of energy.

Birds carry seeds and help plants grow.

Birds are really amazing.

They are connected to everything.

This shows that the Maker of birds, plants, and bugs is the same.

Only Allah can make all these things.

What do birds tell you about Allah?

He knows how to make birds fly.	All-Knowing	Al-Aleem
He gave us many beautiful birds.	The Beautiful	Al-Jameel
He made birds to help plants and animals.	Most Wise	Al-Hakeem
He makes birds many shapes.	The Fashioner	Al-Mussawir
He has the power to make birds from eggs.	Most Powerful	Al-Qadir

Imagine no birds in the sky. No songs, no colors.

Birds are special gifts from Allah.

We must thank Allah for these gifts.

Allah makes birds because He loves us.

Dhikr		Remember, only Allah can make so many pretty birds.
Fikr		Think about how birds are designed to fly.
Shukr		Thank Allah for giving us birds that sing songs.

Character Lessons

Birds teach us.

WORK HARD:

Birds find food and build nests. We must work hard, too.

BE CARING:

Birds help their babies. We help our friends.

BE NICE:

Every bird is different and nice. We must be nice, too.

Teachers notes:

Facilitate discussion with these points: Let's talk about what birds teach us. Birds work well together, showing us how to team up and help each other. They live peacefully with all kinds of birds. They build nests and look after their babies, teaching us to be kind and take care of others. Watching birds helps us learn to live together nicely and care for everyone around us.

Connect with Qur'an

Allah tells us he makes birds fly.

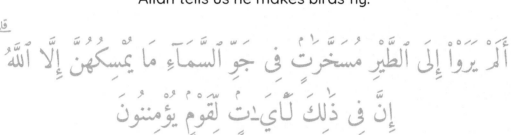

"Do they not see the birds controlled in the atmosphere of the sky? None holds them up except Allah. Indeed, in that are signs for a people who believe."

[Surah al- Nahl, 16: 79]

Watch this video about the flight of birds mentioned in the Quran.

Hadith

This Hadith tells us how to be kind to birds.

Abdullah (ra) reported that the Prophet (pbuh) stopped in a place, and then someone took a bird's eggs, and the bird began to beat its wings around the head of the Prophet (pbuh).

He asked, "Which of you has taken its eggs?" A man said, "Messenger of Allah, I have taken its eggs." The Prophet (pbuh) said, "Return them out of mercy to the bird."

(Al -Adab Al-Mufrad, Hadith # 382)

Du'a

O Allah! Thank you for the lovely birds,

With their colorful wings and happy words.

Keep them safe in the sky so high,

As they sing their songs and fly by.

Activities

Explore

Match the words to the picture.

beak

wing

tail

eye

feet

feathers

See-Think-Wonder

Watch this video to see how birds fly. What did you see?

How can birds fly but we cannot?

How can birds stay in the air for so long?

Arts and Crafts

- Watch this video and find your favorite bird.

- Draw your favorite bird and color it.
- Working in groups, make a bird picture using real feathers.

Compare

Let's Talk

Teacher notes: Facilitate this discussion in small groups.

How long does it take to make an airplane?

Have you ever seen a baby bird hatch out of an egg?

Who teaches a baby bird to fly?

Thinking Cap

 Tick true or false

☐ Some birds cannot fly.

☐ Birds made their wings.

☐ Eggs know how to make a flying body.

☐ Birds can fly because they are clever.

☐ Allah gave birds wings to fly.

Appreciate

Tell your friend three cool things about birds.

Color the name of Allah.

Connect

Draw a picture of the things that birds need. Use the words to help you.

sun   air   insects   plants   animals

What I learned

Draw a picture.

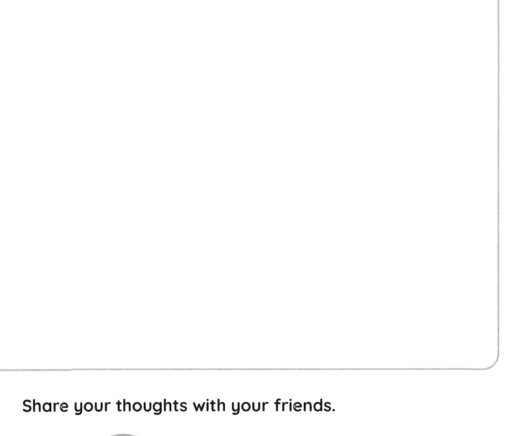

Share your thoughts with your friends.

Delicious Food

Learning Outcomes

After this lesson, learners will be able to:

- Know the types of food.
- Learn that food cannot make itself.
- Understand that Allah made food.
- Learn some names of Allah.
- Know that food is a blessing from Allah.
- Learn some character lessons from food.

First Step · Explore

Grains:

The Energy Foods

"Eat me for energy!"

Proteins:

The Muscle Foods

"I help make muscles strong!"

Fruits:

The Healthy Foods

"I am sweet and good for you!"

Vegatables:

The Healthy Foods

"I keep you healthy!"

Dairy:

The Bone Helpers

"I help bones and teeth grow big and strong!"

All foods are special.

Eat them all to be happy and strong!

Watch this video about healthy food.

Fascinating Facts

Food	Cool facts!
Broccoli	It has more protein than meat.
Potatoes	It was the first food planted in space.
Cucumber	It is made from mostly water.
Carrots	They can be purple and yellow.
Pomegranate	They can have 1000 seeds.

Let's compare real chicken to fake chicken.

A yellow chick comes out of an egg.

It grows into a big chicken.

Scientists make fake chicken from plants.

They made it to taste like real.

They cook it and shape it into nuggets and burgers.

Indeed, fake chicken can taste like real chicken.

Let's look at these videos to see how fake meat is made.

Let's find out who makes real chicken.

Can an egg turn into a chic

No, it cannot.

How do eggs turn into chic

with eyes, wings, and legs?

Let's think together:

- People can make fake chicken, but who makes a real chicken?

- Can scientists make a walking and talking chicken?

- Only someone very knowledgeable and powerful can make a chicken come from an egg.

Who made real chicken?

Facilitate the discussion with these questions: If you put flour, butter, sugar, and eggs in a kitchen with a recipe for making a cake, will the cake get made? No, it will not, even if you leave it there for a long time. Does a pizza get delivered to your house by chance? Or is there a chef working with his helpers to make it? They measure everything carefully and cook at the right temperature. Delicious pizza cannot be made by itself.

4 Fourth Step 🔗 Connect

What does a chick need to live?

A chick needs air and water.

It needs plants, soil, and the sun.

Chickens eat bugs and worms to grow big.

So, the maker of chickens made these things for them.

Only Allah can make them all.

What do chickens tell you about Allah?

He makes chicken and all food.	The Creator	Al-Khaliq
He makes lots of food to keep healthy.	The Provider	Ar-Razzaq
He gives food to everyone.	Most Generous	Al-Kareem
He loves us. He gives us yummy food to enjoy.	Most Loving	Al-Wadud
He knows so much. He can make chicken without an egg and an egg without a chicken.	All-Knowing	Al-Aleem

Facilitate the discussion with these ideas: The sun brings us energy with its warm rays, helping plants grow in the soil. Food is created for plants through photosynthesis as they use water from the ground and carbon dioxide from the air. Animals, like cows and chickens, eat these plants and bring us yummy and healthy food like milk and meat. Animals also are made to help the soil become better by making manure, which gives more nutrients to the plants. Water keeps plants and animals strong and happy. Everything works together, making sure we have the delicious and nutritious food we need. The sun, soil, water, and animals are all made to support and help each other. Allah takes care of beautiful world through them! Let's appreciate this and remember how everything around us is connected so amazingly. It is only a powerful creator that could make this happen.

5 Fifth Step — Appreciate

Allah makes food for us.

Everything you eat was made for you.

It's a special gift.

This shows how much Allah cares for you.

So, thank Him for all the yummy things you eat.

Dhikr — Remember, only Allah could make food.

Fikr — Think how Allah turns soil into yummy food.

Shukr — Thank Allah for giving us delicious food to enjoy.

Teachers notes:

Facilitate the discussion with these ideas: We should be grateful to Allah for providing us with food, just like we appreciate our parents who lovingly prepare delicious meals. When our parents cook amazing food or take us to restaurants, we can feel their love and care for us. Similarly, Allah's blessings are evident in the various foods we enjoy daily. Each bite reminds us of Allah's generosity and love for us, from the colorful fruits and vegetables to the tasty meats and grains. Let's remember to thank Allah for the food we have and show gratitude to our parents for the love and effort they put into making our meals memorable. We can nurture the bond of love and kindness in our families and hearts through appreciation and thankfulness.

Food teaches us to:

SHARE:

Allah is kind and gives us food. We should also be kind and give.

LOVE:

Allah gives us yummy food because He loves us. We should love others.

THANK:

Allah keeps our plates full. We should always say 'thank you'.

Connect with Qur'an

The Qur'an tells us Allah made food for every animal.

وَمَا مِن دَآبَّةٍ فِى ٱلْأَرْضِ إِلَّا عَلَى ٱللَّهِ رِزْقُهَا

"And there is no creature on earth,
but that upon Allah is its provision…"
[SURAH HUD, 11:6]

Hadith

The Prophet (pbuh) tells us we must share food:

"Food for two persons suffices for three, and food for three persons suffices for four."

(MUSLIM)

Du'a

O Allah, you are so true and great,

Thank you for the food on my plate.

Fruits are sweet, veggies are neat,

Chicken and fish are such a treat.

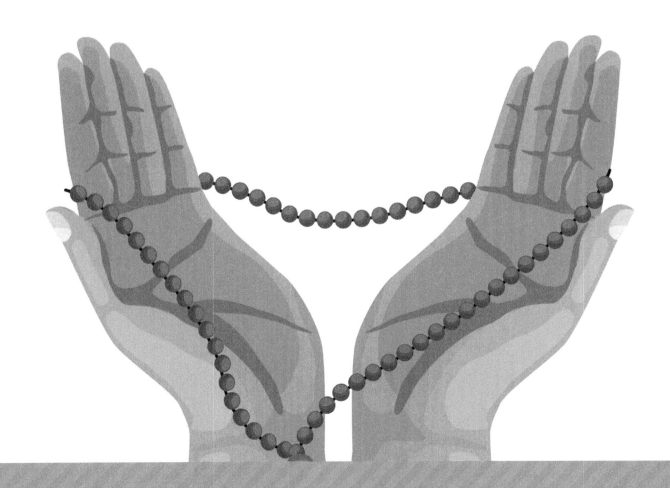

Activities

Explore

Match the food to its group.

| fruit | vegetables | protein | dairy | grains |

See-Think-Wonder

Watch this video about the life of a carrot.
What did you see?

How do dirt and water make carrots?

How does a tiny seed become a tasty carrot?

Compare

- Watch this video and make your own vegetable prints.

- Make artwork using dried fruit and vegetable peels.

Let's Talk

Let's Talk

Teacher notes: Facilitate this discussion in small groups.

Which types of food do you think are healthy?

Why did scientists make fake chicken?

Which do you think is better? Real or fake chicken?

Thinking Cap

 Tick true or false

☐ Scientists can make a chicken that moves like a real one.

☐ Fake chicken is better than real chicken.

☐ Only Allah can make real chickens from nothing.

☐ Eggs do not make themselves.

☐ Food is a blessing.

Appreciate

Tell your friend three yummy foods you like.

Color the name of Allah.

Connect

Draw a picture of some things a chick needs. Use the words to help you.

sun   soil   seeds   insects   grass

What I learned

Draw a picture.

Share your thoughts with your friends.

The Splendid Sun

Learning Outcomes

After this lesson, learners will be able to:

- Know that the Sun is important for life.
- Understand that the Sun cannot make itself.
- Know Allah is the Creator of the Sun.
- Learn some names of Allah.
- Know that the Sun is a blessing for living beings.
- Learn some character lessons from the sun.

Sarah in space

Sarah went to a planetarium.

It was a big round room with stars on the ceiling.

Sarah said, "It's like being in space!"

They watched a show about the Sun.

Sarah learned that the Sun is very hot.

It helps plants grow. It keeps us warm.

We need the Sun.

On the way home, Sarah saw the Sun going down.

Dad stopped the car, and they watched the sunset.

The sky was red, orange, and purple.

The colors were amazing.

Watch this video to learn more.

Fascinating Facts

The Sun	Cool facts!
How big?	The Sun is HUGE! Imagine fitting a million Earths inside it!
How old?	The Sun has had many birthdays. It's 4.5 billion years old!
How far?	If you drove to the Sun in a car, it would take 170 years! Wow!
Light	Sunlight zooms to Earth in 8 minutes.
The fastest	Light is faster than any race car.

Let's compare the Sun to a light bulb.

- It is found in lamps, torches, and lights.
- It lights up rooms, buildings, and streets.
- It needs electricity.
- It needs wires.
- It is small.
- People use it at night.

- It is in the sky.
- It lights up the whole world.
- It has a lot of energy.
- It does not need wires.
- It is huge.
- Plants, animals, humans, Earth, and space all get light from it.

Watch this YouTube video
to see how lightbulbs are made.

Watch this video to see how bulbs were invented.

Let's find out who made the Sun.

Can a lightbulb make itself? No, it cannot.

Now, think of the big, bright Sun.

It's way cooler than a lightbulb!

Can it make itself? No, it cannot.

Who made the Sun shine

so perfectly for Earth?

Let's think together

- In one short hour, Earth gets lots of sunlight.
- This sunlight could light our homes for a year!
- Who is strong enough to make such energy?
- Who knows, we all need this energy?

Who made the Sun?

Facilitate discussion with these ideas: In the video, did you see the hard work and effort that goes into making a lightbulb? It takes a long time for workers to combine all the parts to make a bulb. Then, electricians install them in buildings. Without the hard work of all these people, we wouldn't have the lightbulbs that brighten our world. We also need to switch the lights on and off. But the Sun rises and sets without any involvement from people.

The Sun has a huge amount of energy. It's that energy that plants need to grow. It's that energy that keeps the whole Earth warm. However, lightbulb energy depends upon electricity. When there is a power cut, we use candles! But the Sun never has a power cut. It comes out every day. We receive light through the Sun without any effort from us! How much electricity would be needed to make a lightbulb for the planet? The lightbulb results from years of study by intelligent and skilled individuals. So how can the Sun not have a maker?

 Fourth Step Connect

Can the sun be all by itself?

No, the Sun needs the Earth.

The Sun needs the planets.

Why is the sun important?

We get light from it.

We get heat from it.

We get day and night from it.

The plants get energy from it.

Allah made the Sun for us.

What does the Sun tell you about Allah?

He knows where to put the Sun to help all.	All-Knowing	Al-Aleem
He makes the Sun so big and bright.	All-Powerful	Al-Qadir
He makes sure everywhere on Earth gets sunlight.	Most Wise	Al-Hakeem
He gives us light during the day.	The Light	Al-Noor
He gives us the night to rest.	The Most Merciful	Ar-Rahman

Imagine if there was no night. When would you sleep?

Imagine if there was no day. You would not have green trees and pretty flowers.

The Sun is like a big, bright lightbulb in the sky.

It is a special gift from Allah. Thank Allah for the Sun.

Dhikr		Remember, only Allah could make the shining sun.
Fikr		The Sun always shines, never turning off like a light.
Shukr		Thank Allah for the Sun that lights up our days.

Character Lessons

The Sun teaches us to:

BE A SHINY STAR:

Like the Sun, let's spread joy and love to everyone.

LEND A HAND:

The Sun is made to help plants grow. Let's help everyone!

STAY HAPPY:

Even behind clouds, the Sun shines. So, let's stay happy and keep smiling!

Connect with Qur'an

There is a Surah in the Qur'an called Ash-Shams, which means the Sun. Read and learn it. Think about this verse.

Allah is the Light of the heavens and the earth.

[SURAH NUR:35]

Hadith

This Hadith is a Dua. Learn it and read it every day.

"O Allah, place within my heart light, and upon my tongue light, and within my ears light, and within my eyes light, and place behind me light, and in front of me light, and above me light, and beneath me light. O Allah, bestow upon me light." (Saḥīḥ al-Bukhārī 6316)

Du'a

O Allah, thank You for the Sun so high,

Shining bright and warming the sky.

Guiding and lighting our way.

Alhamdulillah, for its golden ray.

Just like the Sun, let me shine bright,

Helping others with your Might.

Activities

Explore

Match the pictures to the correct word.

sun	star	moon	earth	solar system

See-Think-Wonder

Watch this video about Sunrise and Sunset.

What did you see?

What does it make you think of?

How can Sunrise and Sunset happen?

- Make artwork of the Sun using yellow and orange tissue paper.
- Group work: Make a model of the solar system.

Compare

Let's Talk

Teacher notes: Facilitate this discussion in small groups.

What would happen if there was no Sun?

Can scientists ever make something like the Sun?

How do you benefit from the Sun?

Thinking Cap

 Tick true or false

☐ The Sun makes heat by itself.

☐ The Sun makes light by itself.

☐ We can live without the Sun.

☐ Allah made the Sun.

☐ Allah makes light and heat in the Sun.

Connect

Draw a picture of the things the sun needs. Use the words to help you.

(sun) (light) (space) (earth) (stars)

Color the name of Allah.

Appreciate

Tell your friend three fun things about the Sun.

What I learned?

Draw a picture.

Share your thoughts with your friends.

Magnificent Moon

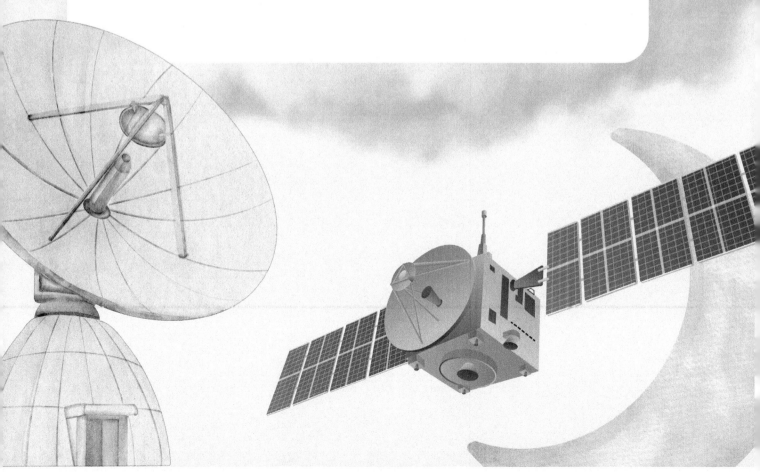

Learning Outcomes

After this lesson, learners will be able to:

- Know the importance of the Moon.
- Know that the Moon cannot make itself.
- Know that Allah made the Moon.
- Learn some names of Allah.
- Know that the Moon is a blessing of Allah.
- Learn some character lessons from the Moon.

Ramadhan Moon

"It's Ramadhan," said Mum.

Adam saw a tiny curve in the sky. "It's the new Moon!"

Grandpa said, "The Moon does not have its own light.

It gets light from the Sun. As the month passes,

you will see it get big and bright. Then it will get small and disappear."

Adam learned that the Moon takes one month to go around the Earth.

When the Moon is close to the Sun, its surface is hot. At night, it is cold.

Every night, Adam watched the Moon. It got bigger and bigger.

Then, one day, it was a big circle. It was so bright.

When Ramadhan ended, the Moon was gone.

Adam remembered what Grandpa said.

He knew the Moon would come back. He smiled, thinking of Eid!

Let's look at this video to find out more.

Let's look at this video
to learn about the Moon's phases.

Fascinating Facts

The Moon	Cool Fact
It is the Earth's friend.	It moves around the Earth.
It is very far.	It would take three days to get there in a spaceship.
It bounces light from the Sun.	Light from the Moon reaches Earth in a second.
It has weak gravity.	If you jumped on the Moon, you would jump very high.
If you weigh 60 pounds on the Earth.	You would weigh only 10 pounds on the Moon

Let's compare the Moon to a man-made satellite.

Moon

IIt is made from rock.

It is huge!

It does not need any power.

It goes around the Earth so high.

Like a calendar in the sky.

Satellite

It is made from metal.

Some are small, like cars. Some are big, like buses.

It needs power to work.

They help us talk to each other.

They help us find out about the weather.

Watch the video to learn about satellites.
(From 2min 44 seconds)

123

Watch this video to see how satellites are built:

Let's find out who made the Moon.

Can a toy build itself? No! Someone has to make it.

Satellites are big machines in space. Scientists make them.

Can the Moon make itself? No, it cannot.

Let's think together

- Who put the Moon in the perfect spot to give us light at night?
- Who made the Moon take one month to go around Earth?
- Why doesn't the Moon fly away into the sky?
- Who could be strong enough to create the Moon?

Who is the Maker of the Moon?

Teachers notes:

Facilitate discussion with these ideas: How does the Moon move in the sky with such precision? The Moon looks different each night and helps us calculate time. How does it maintain its distance and speed? Why does it not rotate like the Earth and the Sun? Can you imagine a world without the Moon? How would it be different? How many things would change without the Moon? It's amazing how Allah's creations work together in perfect harmony.

What does the Moon need?

Can the Moon be by itself? No, it needs the Earth.

It also needs the Sun and planets.

The Moon, stars, and Sun are like a team in the sky.

They help make the sky light up the night.

The Sun brings energy to the Earth.

Everything in space works together.

So, whoever made the Sun and Earth

also made the Moon.

Only Allah can make all of them.

Teachers notes:

Imagine the Moon and stars as a team floating together in space. They are put together to make everything in the sky beautiful and bright. Each has an important job, like shining light and giving energy to each other and the universe. The Earth needs the Moon, just as it needs the Sun. So, we can see that everything in space is connected and need each other. So, the One who makes the Sun and the Earth must also be the Creator of the Moon. The Moon is designed to brighten the entire Earth, reflecting the Sun's light and providing a gentle glow at night. The Moon affects the tides, helping life on Earth. Who has the knowledge and power to make the Moon travel around the Earth? Who has the wisdom to employ the Moon for many purposes. It is only Allah.

What does the Moon tell you about Allah?

He gave us the Moon to help us know the Islamic months.	The Loving	Al-Wadud
He only has the power move the Moon around the Earth.	All-Powerful	Al-Qadir
He makes the Moon to light up our night.	Most Wise	Al-Hakeem
He is the one who gives us soft Moonlight.	The Light	Al-Noor
He is kind for giving night animals moonlight to find food.	The Most Merciful	Ar-Rahman

 **Fifth Step** **Appreciate**

What if there was no Moon to light up our night?

It would be so dark!

The Moon tells us about Ramadhan.

The Moon's glow is a special gift.

Thank Allah for the Moon.

Dhikr	Remember only Allah can make a big, shiny Moon.
Fikr	Think how the Moon is like a big nightlight in the sky.
Shukr	Thank Allah for making the Moon to help us.

The moon teaches us to:

SHINE BRIGHT:

Just like the Moon lights the night; we can shine by being happy and kind.

STICK TOGETHER:

The Moon always stays near Earth. We should stick with our friends.

ALWAYS ON TIME:

The Moon shows up when it's supposed to, reminding us to be on time too.

Connect with Qur'an

Allah tells us about the Moon 28 times in the Quran.

هُوَ الَّذِي جَعَلَ الشَّمْسَ ضِيَاءً وَالْقَمَرَ نُورًا وَقَدَّرَهُ مَنَازِلَ لِتَعْلَمُوا عَدَدَ السِّنِينَ وَالْحِسَابَ مَا خَلَقَ اللَّهُ ذَلِكَ إِلَّا بِالْحَقِّ يُفَصِّلُ الْآيَاتِ لِقَوْمٍ يَعْلَمُونَ

"It is He who made the Sun a shining light and the Moon a derived light and determined for its phases – that you may know the number of years and account [of time]. Allah has not made this except in truth. He details the signs for people who know".

[Surat Yunus, 10:5]

Hadith

The Prophet (pbuh) said, "Fast on sighting it (the new Moon) and break it on sighting it. But if (due to clouds) the actual position of the month is concealed from you, you should then count thirty (days)".

Watch this lovely video about the Ramadhan Moon.

Du'a

Moon up high, glowing in the night,

Thank you, Allah, for this lovely light.

Moon so round, changing its face,

Telling us life has its own pace.

Be patient, be kind, just like the moon,

Allah's blessings will come soon.

A c t i v i t i e s

Color in the picture to show each phase of the Moon.

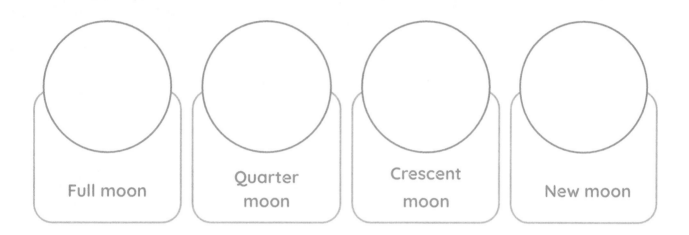

Full moon

Quarter moon

Crescent moon

New moon

See-Think-Wonder

Watch this video about how the Moon appears from Earth. What did you see?

How does the Earth spin and the Moon move?

How does this system work correctly all the time?

Arts and Crafts

- Make a textured Moon picture using different materials.
- Group work: Make a long poster of the Moon phases using aluminum foil.

Compare

Let's talk

Teacher notes: Facilitate this discussion in small groups.

Why do we need the Moon?

How do satellites help us?

What if there was no Moon?

Thinking Cap

 Tick true or false

- ☐ Eid starts with the sighting of the new Moon.

- ☐ The Moon has its own light.

- ☐ The Moon was made by nature.

- ☐ Allah made the Moon.

- ☐ The Moon travels around the Earth by itself.

Appreciate

Tell your friend three fun things about the Moon.

Color the name of Allah.

Connect

Draw a picture of the things the Moon needs. Use the words to help you.

sun   earth   space   stars

What I learned?

Draw a picture.

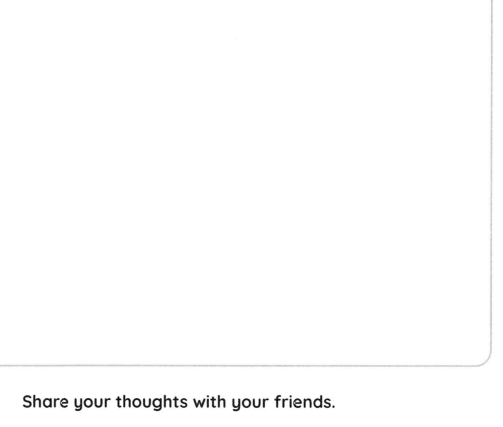

Share your thoughts with your friends.

Wonderful Weather

Learning Outcomes

After this lesson, learners will be able to:

- Recall the types of weather.
- Know that weather cannot make itself.
- Understand Allah made all types of weather.
- Learn some names of Allah.
- Know that weather is a blessing from Allah.
- Learn some character lessons from weather.

Weather Wonders

Hello! I'm a raindrop.
When I'm with my friends, we are called a cloud.
Rain is sent from clouds.

Do you feel the wind?
It moves leaves and trees.
It can bring smells from far away.

Some days are Sunny and warm.

When it is cold, raindrops are made into snow!
Snow is fun for playing with friends.

Watch this video about types of weather.

Fascinating Facts

Did you know?

Super-Hot!	Lightning is super-hot, even hotter than the Sun.
Busy!	Thunderstorms happen a lot, every single day.
Huge!	Some raindrops are big like bugs.
Shady!	The first umbrellas were for shade, not rain.
Colorful!	Sunlight and raindrops together give a pretty rainbow.

2 Second Step ⚖ Compare

Let's compare the weather to heaters and air conditioners.

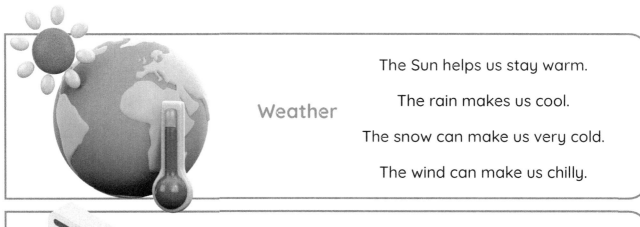

Weather

The Sun helps us stay warm.

The rain makes us cool.

The snow can make us very cold.

The wind can make us chilly.

Heater

Heats homes and buildings.

-

The heater can warn us.

-

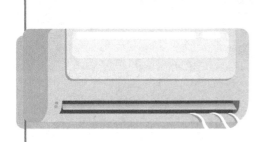

Air
Conditioner

-

It makes us cool on a hot day.

-

It makes us cool on a hot day.

Outside, the Sun and wind help us feel good. Inside, we use machines.
Watch these videos to know more.

Cooling Devices

Here is a video about making
a cooling device at home.

Heating Devices

Look at this video to see
how to make a heater.

Third Step   ⓠ Question

Let's find out who made the weather.

Did the Sun decide to shine all on its own?

No, the Sun cannot think.

Can the wind choose when to blow?

No, the wind cannot think.

Does a heater decide to warm us?

Does an AC decide to cool us?

No, they cannot think.

Machines need people to make them.

Do wind, rain, clouds, and snow make themselves?

Let's think together:

- Why is the weather warmer on some days?
- Why does the wind feel different sometimes?
- People made heaters and ACs

Who made the weather?

4 Fourth Step 🔗 Connect

What makes up the weather?

Earth is like a big home.

Some places need Sun.

Some places need rain.

Some areas have snow.

Some places have wind.

Someone made all these things perfect for us.

Everything, so neatly in its place,

Only Allah has big power to make them nice.

What does the weather tell you about Allah?

He is the one who made all types of weather.	The Creator	Al-Khaliq
He gives us warm and cool weather.	The Most Merciful	Ar-Rahman
He gives the right weather for plants and animals.	The Most Wise	Al-Hakeem
Only He has the power to make it very hot or very cold.	The Most Powerful	Al-Qadir
He knows everything. Only He can change water into rain, hail, and snow.	All-Knowing	Al-Aleem

Earth's weather is a special thing,
Other planets are not good to live.
Some are too hot, some freezing at night,
But the Earth is just perfectly right!
Weather is made to help plants grow up tall,
For that we shall thank Allah, the maker of all.
Don't litter, keep the Earth neat and fine,
Plant trees and flowers, let them shine.
So, when the Sun shines or rain comes your way,
Thank Allah for the weather, every day!

Dhikr		Remember that only Allah could make the weather.
Fikr		Think how Allah makes the Sunny days, rainy afternoons, and snowy mornings!
Shukr		Thank Allah for rain, snow, wind, and the Sun.

Let us listen to this song to thank Allah for everything:

Character Lessons

The weather teaches us to:

BE PATIENT:

Like waiting for rain to stop.

HELP EACH OTHER:

Like the Sun, wind, rain, and snow do.

SPREAD SMİLES:

Like sunny days do after rain.

Connect with Qur'an

Allah tells us how he changes the weather.

اللّٰهُ الَّذِى يُرْسِلُ الرِّيَـٰحَ فَتُثِيرُ سَحَابًا فَيَبْسُطُهُ فِى السَّمَآءِ كَيْفَ يَشَآءُ وَيَجْعَلُهُ كِسَفًا فَتَرَى الْوَدْقَ يَخْرُجُ مِنْ خِلَـٰلِهِ ۖ فَإِذَآ أَصَابَ بِهِۦ مَن يَشَآءُ مِنْ عِبَادِهِۦٓ إِذَا هُمْ يَسْتَبْشِرُونَ

"It is Allah who sends the winds, and they stir the clouds and spread them in the sky however He wills, and He makes them fragments so you see the rain emerge from within them. And when He causes it to fall upon whom He wills of His servants, immediately they rejoice."

[SURAH RUM: 30, 48]

Hadith

This Hadith tells us that only Allah can send the rain.
Abdullah ibn Zayd (ra) reported I saw the Prophet,
(pbuh) one day go out to pray for rain.

(BUKHARI & MUSLIM)

Du'a

Raindrops fall, soft and light,

Snow makes the ground so white.

Wind whispers secrets in our ear,

Allah's helps are always near.

Be thankful for each, every day,

For the weather, let's kneel and pray.

Activities

Explore

Match the picture to the correct word.

windy	cloudy	rainy	snowy	sunny

See-Think-Wonder

Watch this video about a rainbow. What did you see?

How much power is needed to make a rainbow?

How can a rainbow form in the sky?

Arts and Crafts

- Make a rainbow with colored tissue paper.
- Group work: Make artwork of different types of weather on one large chart paper.

Compare

Let's talk:

Teacher notes: Facilitate this discussion in small groups.

What would happen if it was hot all the time?

What would happen if the rain never stopped?

What would happen if the snow never melted?

Question

✓ **Tick true or false** ✗

☐ Rain and snow form and fall themselves.

☐ Clouds give us water because they care.

☐ Clouds and the air decide together to make snow.

☐ A raindrop can be the size of a housefly.

☐ All weather is a blessing.

Appreicate

Tell your friend three fun things about the weather.

Color the name of Allah.

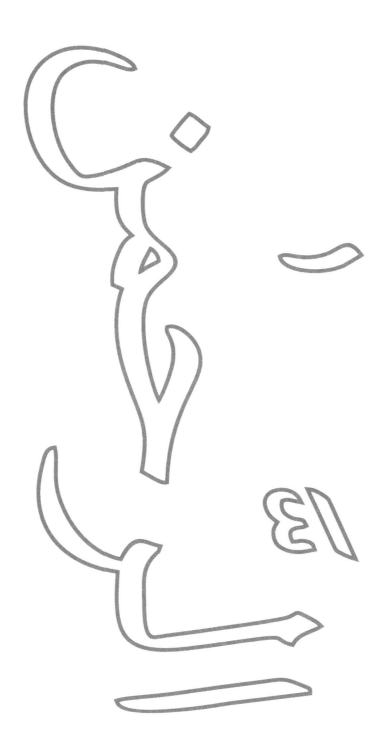

Connect

Let's find some things that the weather is connected to.

Draw a picture of the things the weather needs. Use the words to help you.

| sun | rain | snow | wind | clouds |

Draw a picture.

Share your thoughts with your friends.

Marvelous Materials

Learning Outcomes

After this lesson, learners will be able to:

- Explore different types of material.
- Understand that materials cannot make themselves.
- Understand that it is Allah who makes materials.
- Learn some names of Allah.
- Know that materials are a blessing.
- Learn some character lessons from materials.

Materials around us

Things around us are made of different stuff, and each is special!

Example	How It Feels	Material
Toy car	Hard & Smooth	Plastic
Teddy bear	Soft	Fabric
Kitchen spoon	Cold & Shiny	Metal
Grandma's sweater	Warm & Cozy	Wool
Wooden blocks	Rough	Wood
Pages in a book	Smooth & Thin	Paper

Look at this video about materials.

Fascinating Facts

Did you know that we get many things from different trees?

1. Maple trees bring to us sweet syrup for pancakes.
2. Apple trees bring to us juicy apples to eat.
3. Banana trees bring to us tasty bananas to snack on.
4. Coconut trees bring to us yummy milk to drink.
5. Rubber trees bring things to make balloons and car tires.

2 Second Step ⚖ Compare

Let's compare wood with plastic made by humans.

Wood	Plastic
Made from trees.	Made in factories from oil.
Used for furniture, houses, and paper.	Used for toys, cups, and furniture.
Good for soil.	Cause pollution.

Watch this video to find out how plastic is made in a factory.

Third Step Question

Let's find out who made wood.

Can a seed know it needs to grow into a tree?

No, it does not.

Can roots make a tree grow?

No, they cannot.

Can plastic make itself?

No, it cannot.

A team works in a factory to make plastic.

Let's think together:

• How can different seeds make different trees?
• Why do trees need roots, soil, water, and Sunlight to grow?
• Only someone very wise and strong can make trees.

Who makes trees? Who makes rocks? Who makes metals?

Teachers notes:

Facilitate the discussion with these questions: If a plastic-making factory needs an architect to design it and a manager to run it, and resources must arrive through transport, what about the sustenance of trees? Who is the designer and provider of trees? Who is the manager? Who facilitates the process of plastic making? Can it be nature that doesn't think or plan?

Everything around us works together!

The Sun helps plants grow.

Trees bring us wood for toys, paper for drawing, and sweet sap.

Rocks bring us metal for cars and glass windows.

All these things are given to us by Allah because he knows what we need.

Only He can make all these special things for us.

What do materials tell you about Allah?

He is the one who made many materials.	The Creator	Al-Khaliq
He makes trees grow. He gives us lots of good things from them.	The Sustainer	Ar-Rabb
He is kind. He gives us many things for free. We make stuff from them.	The Most Generous	Al-Kareem
He alone has the power to make different materials.	The Most Powerful	Al-Qadir
He gives us strong wood and metals.	The Most Strong	Al-Qawwi

Look around your home.

Do you see different materials? Some things are hard. Some are soft. They all help us! We have soft blankets to keep warm. We eat with metal spoons. We sit on wooden chairs. We ride in big metal cars to fun places! Can you see that they are amazing gifts?

Dhikr		Remember that only Allah is the Creator of all materials.
Fikr		Think how Allah makes the amazing types of materials for different uses.
Shukr		Thank Allah for the useful materials that make life easier.

Character Lessons

Materials teach us to:

BE STRONG:

Wood and metal are strong and tough. We should be strong, too.

SHARE WITH OTHERS:

Trees share with everyone. We should share, too.

BE HELPFUL:

Materials are made to help. We should be helpful, too.

Connect with Qur'an

The Qur'an tells us that Allah has made trees and all other materials.

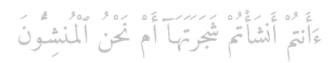

Is it you who produce its trees, or is it We Who do so?

[AL WAQIAH, 56: 72]

Hadith

The Prophet (pbuh) tells us about the gift of trees:

"There is none amongst the Muslims who plants a tree or sows seeds, and then a bird, or a person or an animal eats from it, but is regarded as a charitable gift for him."

(BUKHARI)

Du'a

O Allah, with heart so pure, I say:

Thank you for all materials, every day.

Wood, metal, cloth, and even clay,

Help me in life, in a special way.

So, guide me to care and use,

These gifts of yours, not to abuse.

Activities

Match the picture to the correct word.

| metal | wood | glass | plastic | fabric |

See-Think-Wonder

Watch this video about beautiful trees. What did you see?

What do you think about the many types of trees?

How do you think they grow so tall?

- Make tree bark rubbings and then paste some leaves to make a forest.
- **Group work:** Use different types of cloth, such as silk, wool, and cotton, to make a design.

Compare

Let's talk:

Teacher notes: Facilitate this discussion in small groups.

What would happen if there was no wood or metal?

How would life be if there was only one type of material

to make furniture and all the things we need?

Thinking Cap

✓ **Tick true or false** ✗

☐ Metals are shiny.

☐ Paper is made by nature.

☐ Trees grow because of luck.

☐ Wood is a gift to make furniture.

☐ Materials are not important.

Appreciate

Tell your friend three things about materials that make you happy.

Color the name of Allah.

Draw a picture of materials Allah made for us. Use the words to help you.

metal   plastic   wood   wool   paper

What I learned?

Draw a picture.

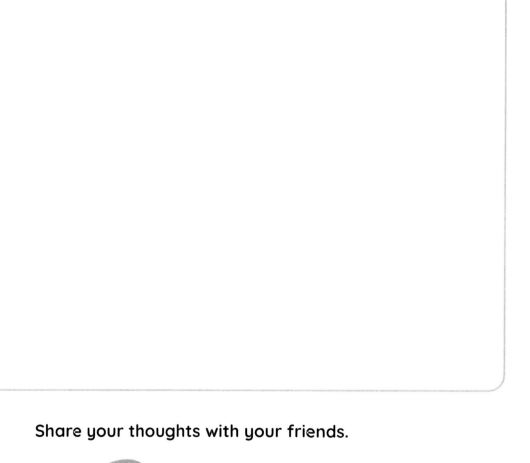

Share your thoughts with your friends.

Happy Habitats

Learning Outcomes

After this lesson, learners will be able to:

- Learn the importance of habitats.
- Understand that nature cannot make habitats.
- Understand that it is Allah who made all habitats.
- Learn some names of Allah.
- Know that habitats are a blessing.
- Learn some character lessons from hapitats.

Forest friends

Dara, the deer, Ray, the rabbit, and Woody, the woodpecker, lived happily.

The tall trees kept them cool in summer and warm in winter.

Dara munched grass. She slept under the shade of the tree.

The forest ground was soft.

Ray dug a home. It was his safe spot!

Woody lived in a big tree. He liked eating bugs.

The forest was home for all.

They had food. It was safe.

They were happy.

Watch this video to learn more.

Fascinating Facts

Did You Know?	
Trees Everywhere!	Forests are a big part of Earth.
Super Big Rainforest	The Amazon is a giant jungle with many trees.
Big Forest Friend	The African elephant is really big!
Tiny Forest Friend	The bumblebee bat is so small, like a tiny toy!
Old, Old Trees	Some trees in forests are very old!

Let's compare the forest habitat to your home.

Your Home	Forest Habitat
You live with your family.	Animals live with their groups.
Has everything you need.	Has everything animals need.
Keeps you safe.	Offers animals a place to live.
Protects from weather.	Shields from rain, snow, & the Sun.

Watch this video about homes:

Let's find out who made the forest habitat.

Did your home make itself?

Did bricks decide to make walls?

What about a forest habitat?

Did soil, plants, and trees decide to make a forest?

Let's think together

- Did the Earth decide to grow lots of trees by itself?
- Someone made your house, so someone made the forest for animals.
- If your house was built, the forest was built too!

Who made the amazing habitat of the forest?

What do forests need?

Forests need the Sun, soil, plants, and trees.

They also need rivers for water.

Everything in the forest is connected.

Earth has many forests.

Forests are homes for animals.

Who can know how to make a wonderful forest?

Only Allah could make forests perfect homes for many animals.

What does the forest habitat tell you about Allah?

He knows everything that plants need.	All-Knowing	AL-ALEEM
He gives food to all creatures.	The Provider	AR-RAZZAQ
He gives life to everything from nothing.	The Giver of Life	AL-MUHYI
He made everything.	The Creator	AL-KHALIQ
He is an amazing designer, making millions of types of plants.	The Fashioner	AL-MUSAWWIR

Forests are pretty.

There are lots of plants and animals.

Forests are a gift.

Thank Allah for them.

Dhikr		Remember Allah alone could make forests.
Fikr		Think about how Allah make forests to give animals food and shelter.
Shukr		Thank Allah for the gift of forests.

Character Lessons

Forests teach us to:

BE PEACEFUL:

Forests are peaceful. Make your home peaceful.

PROTECT OTHERS:

Forests keep animals safe. We should take care of those who need help.

BE HELPFUL:

Plants and animals help each other in forests. We should help friends and family.

Connect with Qur'an

Allah tells us about homes in the Qur'an.

وَٱللَّهُ جَعَلَ لَكُم مِّنۢ بُيُوتِكُمۡ سَكَنًا

And Allah has made your homes a place to rest.

[SURAH AN NAHL, 16: 80]

Hadith

This Hadith tells us about how we can get a permanent house in Jannah.

Narrated by Abu Umamah (ra), The Prophet (pbuh) said: I guarantee a house in the surroundings of Paradise for a man who avoids quarreling even if he were in the right, a house in the middle of Paradise for a man who avoids lying even if he were joking, and a house in the upper part of Paradise for a man who made his character good.(Abu Dawud)

Du'a

O Allah, thank you for places, big and small,

For habitats that house creatures all.

Like homes give us safety, love, and care,

Animals too have places to live and share.

Activities

Explore

Match the animal to its habitat.

See-Think-Wonder

Watch this video about beautiful forest habitats.

What did you see?

What do you think about this habitat?

How can a forest can be home to many creatures?

Arts and Crafts

- Select any habitat and use art materials to make it.
- Draw your house and color it.

Compare

Let's talk:

Teacher notes: Facilitate this discussion in small groups.

What things are needed in every habitat?

Which things in your home can you not live without?

Who could know what type of habitat every animal need?

Thinking Cap

✓ Tick true or false ✗

☐ Forests cover half of the Earth's land area.

☐ Animals and humans need food and shelter.

☐ Animals are lucky to have forests.

☐ Animals choose their habitats.

☐ A forest is a blessing of Allah.

Appreciate

Tell your friend three things about materials that make you happy.

Color the name of Allah.

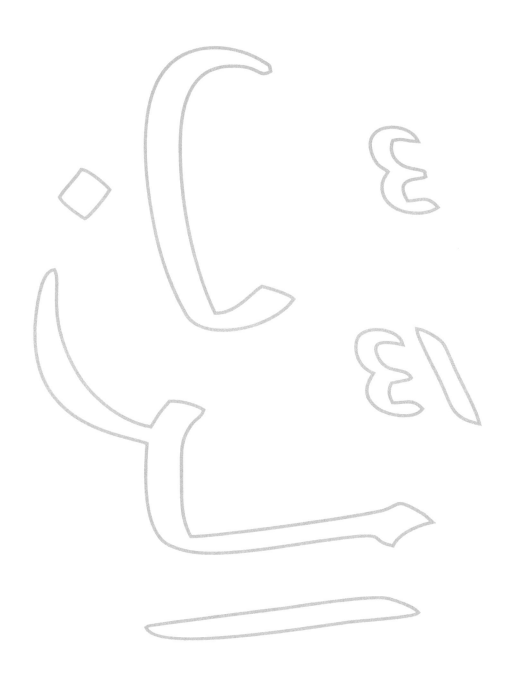

Draw a picture of a forest habitat. Use the words to help you.

food   tree   water   plants   grass   ground

What I learned?

Draw a picture.

Share your thoughts with your friends.

Testimonials from Educators
at 5D Pilot Schools

"Our students were thoroughly fascinated by the content matter of the lessons. They enjoyed the steps involved in 5D thinking and continually made connections with Allah as the creator of everything in the universe. This enabled them to learn the 99 names of Allah and their relevance to the topics taught. Furthermore, students learned valuable lessons that enhanced their already existing morals and values from the 5D program. Finally, they appreciated Allah's creations and gave special thanks to Allah."

Dr. Rashida Khan, HOD, Elementary section

Al Falaah School (5D Pilot School), South Africa

"The wonderful thing about 5D Thinking is that it allows teachers to engage with a conceptual framework based on an Islamic worldview and thereby support children to engage with scientific concepts using that framework. This is conducive to holistically integrating Science education and Tarbiyah."

Dr Farah Ahmed, Research Fellow, University of Cambridge

Director of Education, Islamic Shakhsiyah Foundation UK

"The 5D model has enhanced and enriched our curriculum at the Islamic Shakhsiyah Foundation. Our children can now make more meaningful and deeper links with Allah (swt) as the creator of the universe and understand their purpose as stewards of the earth."

Sajeada Ahmed, Acting Head Teacher

Shakhsiyah School UK (5D pilot school)

"The 5D approach is an inquiry-based model to develop Aqeedah and rationality among young learners. I am delighted to share that 5D aided in the development of curiosity, leading towards contentment and nullifying secular educational ideas. The model gives a clear framework for conducting lessons and making science fun and engaging."

Dr. Fareehah Khalid, Principal, House of Wisdom (5D pilot school), Pakistan

Testimonials from Educators
Attending 5D Training

"The 5D program is an amazing vitamin shot that I was blessed to take. It opened my eyed on the secular resources that I was using while teaching science. Amazing and highly recommended program."

Manal Hilal

Science MYP teacher, Jeddah, SA

"Muslim educators have the trust of the community and amanah from Allah to not only convey information to the youth, but also to transform. This 5D Program has been a transformational experience for me and I look forward to bringing it to my school and community."

Salar Rasoul

Director of Religious Affairs - ISNA Schools, UK

"The 5D Thinking training was extremely beneficial and enlightening. Islamic schools have been trying to integrate Islam with academic subjects and come up with various character education programs but haven't been able to do so 100%. The 5D Model is the answer to both integration and character development. I think every Islamic school globally should be implementing this model! I am so blessed to have been a part of the first teacher training in Istanbul and cannot wait to implement it at my school in Canada insha'Allah."

Ghazala Choudhary

Principal, Tarbiyah Learning Academy, Canada

"This is a must for Muslim educators of the 21st century. It is about a holistic and transformative approach to teaching and learning. It is the awakening and reviving of the hearts and minds of the ummah. The 5D can be seamlessly integrated. It encompasses all the domains of learning. Teaches students to question claims and seek truth."

Mona Egeh,

Principal, Ottawa Islamic School, Canada

IIK and 5D Thinking Team
The Institute of Integrated Knowledge (IIK)

Located in Hartford, CT, the Institute of Integrated Knowledge (IIK) was founded in 2021 by a group of international scholars. It aims to be a center for advanced study, research, and community outreach, catering to individuals from a rich tapestry of cultural and professional backgrounds. With a vision rooted in interdisciplinary exploration, the Institute seeks to bridge the wisdom found in both Islamic scholarly and scientific traditions with modern arts and sciences. By fostering this blend of ancient knowledge and contemporary insights, IIK strives to unveil deeper meanings and purposes of existence and the human experience. For more information about IIK, please visit:

www.iiknowledge.org

Dr. Necati Aydin is a professor of economics specializing in well-being and the moral economy from a multidisciplinary perspective. He also serves as the vice president of the Institute of Integrated Knowledge. He holds two doctoral degrees, one in education and the other in economics. He spent a decade in the USA as a researcher, completing over forty research projects before commencing his academic career. He is the author of nine books and has translated two, co-authored three, and published numerous peer-reviewed articles. His work includes several publications within the realm of the Islamic moral economy. His recent work includes a book published by Routledge titled "Said Nursi and Science in Islam: Character Building through the Mana-i Harfi Approach" and another titled "3D of Happiness: Pleasure, Meaning, and Spirituality". Collaborating with various scholars, he has developed the 5D thinking model for the integration of knowledge. He is also the project leader of a science workbook series that encourages the exploration of God's hidden signs in the scientific understanding of the universe.

Uzma Ahmed is Director of Education and Training at the Institute of Integrated knowledge, Hartford, USA. She has designed the 5Dkids program. Uzma Ahmed holds a BSc Hons. In International Relations from the University of London and an MA in International Relations from Queen Mary University of London. She has also completed a Diploma in Islamic Education from the International Online University with a broad range of Islamic disciplines. She has worked as an Educational Consultant, Primary school Principal, Curriculum developer, Researcher in Islamic education, and Teacher trainer for schools in the UK and Pakistan for 25 years. She conducts short courses for Quran, Sirah, Islamic history, and personal development. She is a public speaker on Contemporary Islamic issues in the Muslim world. She has authored primary level English textbooks and Reading books and regularly writes material for homeschoolers and Islamic courses for children of all ages on many topics with a focus on Islamic history and Tarbiyah.

Saba Irshad Ansari is a Senior Research Fellow at the Department of Islamic Studies, Aligarh Muslim University, India. She is a faculty topper at the Faculty of Social Sciences, AMU. She also holds two gold medals for the years 2016 and 2018. Her main area of interest is Muslim theology and contemporary Islamic thought. She is also a Director of the Existence and Meaning Programs at the Institute of Integrated Knowledge, Hartford, CT, USA. She has co-instructed the 5D kids' program in 2021. She is a public speaker on Islam and interfaith peace dialogue in India.

5D Thinking Web Portal

We invite you to explore the enriching content on the 5D Thinking Web Portal:

www.5dthinking.org

Here, you will find the thought-provoking 5D Thinking Magazine and a variety of educational materials designed to broaden your perspective. Additionally, this portal offers you the opportunity to contribute your unique insights as a 5D author. Join our community of curious and engaged learners in shaping a multidimensional approach to knowledge. Visit us and begin your journey into the enriching world of 5D Thinking.

Printed in Great Britain
by Amazon

46538673R00110